Before The
World
Moves On

Nathaniel Terrell

WARRINGTON

Danbury, Connecticut

Before the World Moves On
Copyright © 2025 by Nathaniel Terrell

Published by Warrington Publishing
Danbury, CT
www.warringtonpublishing.com

All rights reserved. No part of this publication may be reproduced, stored in a retrieval system, or transmitted by any means – electronic, mechanical, photographic (photocopying), recording, or otherwise – without prior permission in writing from the author. For such requests, contact the publisher directly at www.warringtonpublishing.com.

Printed in the United States of America

First Edition

ISBN: 978-1-944972-56-1 (paperback)
978-1-944972-55-4 (ebook)
978-1-944972-66-0 (hardcover)

Cover designed by Warrington Design Studio

This book is a work of fiction. Names, characters, places, and incidents either are products of the author's imagination or are used fictitiously. Any resemblance to actual persons, living or dead, events, or locales is entirely coincidental.

This collection is dedicated to
Jason Sylvester Singletary (Jay Sly Sing)

Your memory, impact, and work live on
Rest easy, my brother and friend

Poetry Collections by Nathaniel Terrell

Is There Not a Cause?
Before the World Moves On

Order of Content

Timeline
Soulmates
Dream catcher
Conflict
Audition
Broken crutch
Seconds left
Sequel
Oh, hell no!
Prayer
Tactics
Thirteen to one
Wait what?
Diary
Cancerous culture
Slow burn
Spirit of expectation
Open door
Vanity
In need
What's it worth?
Within
Early Autumn
Yeah that's right

Order of Content, continued

Another day
She is
March on
A window in heaven
Can't call it
Day one
The thing is this
Eclipse
No such thing
Devil may cry
Finite bliss
Unanswered
Nightcap
Great escape
One more chance
Free game
Discovery
Community
Road trip
Backlash
Old man
Taking the risk
Stories, anthems, dreams
Patience, devotion, time

Order of Content, continued

You already know
Did not
No promises
Anecdotally
Nonstop
Short term
Fortitude
Long one
If I ruled the world
Facing Jericho
Poker face
Deadline
On my way
Open mic
Jaded
Strategy
Interlude of the sad man
Alluring situations
Respectfully
Happy as hell
Stay
Whiplash
Worldwide
Lessons and Blessings

Order of Content, continued

Conditioned
Eulogy
Born again
Clarity cuts
Samantha smile
The grave equator
In remembrance of
Pretty eyes
Get ready
Reasons
Summer
Anti
Paradox
Never
Old dog barking
Love note
Against the flow
Becoming
I could be wrong
Past time

Timeline

At this stage in my life
My question with almost everything I face is

What am I to learn from this situation to make me better?
or, how can I use this opportunity to grow?

Why, is now less of importance to me
how, usually always piques my interest

I am not ashamed of much
but regret, now that's a whole different story

I want to share with you
how I truly feel

But I care about your feelings
so I pretend, I am at a loss for words

Deception plays out minute by minute
but if I bite my tongue

I cannot admonished
for claiming that, what is proven to be true, is not

I wish I had been strong enough to not cheat
I wish I never developed an infatuation for stealing

Nights like this, I miss my team

I hate that I paid little attention to all the hints
on that warm autumn night

I fear that it may be too late…

I can honestly say that
I am not ashamed of much

But regret, now that's a whole different story

Soul mates

We came to the terms
that we can never be together

I am unable to drink away
all the love, I have for you

Oh, the games we've played
we were also vulnerable with and open to each other

I can read your facial expressions
you know my darkest secrets

We've upheld each other
through hard times and disappointments

Soulmates creatively. sparred intellectually,
satisfaction in exceeding pleasures as part-time lovers

Enjoyed deep conversations, had passionate
disagreements
and possess an authentic spiritual connection

I would alway, hold you too close and for too long,
with those sweet body to body hugs

Soft mahogany-toned skin, with a great sense of humor,
emotionally intelligent, the best-friend I ever had

You call my mother ma
I address your mother the same

It hurt like hell
watching Pop march you down the aisle

It was a lovely day, you looked so happy
you bore the resemblance of an angel

Your smile got brighter when you saw my smile,
I would not let you see my tears

It took me awhile to accept the reality
that we will never be together

Woman, I have always known
I won't ever love another
the way that I love you

Dream catcher

Got called in to work
on my day off
to clean toilets and push a broom

I made plans to spend time with family
but first, I must provide
consequently ruining our afternoon

My probation officer don't play
past mistakes have made life hard

Making just above minimum wage
I depend on an unreliable car

I thank God for blessing me with a gift
lack of interest, kept me just above average in school

Every day, I hear these yuppies talk
and they sound like educated fools

My situation could be worse, I could have nothing
so, I clean their mess day after day

I humble myself and do the dirty work
earning an honest day's pay

I write stories, poems, anthems and songs
and answer submission calls

No, I have not reached my goal yet
however, I am walking tall

Through God's grace and hard work
I've made it this far
I will be successful soon

Until then, I will put on these gloves
clean that toilet and push this broom

Conflict

Mediocrity births complacency
only the exceptional conquer quests

                        It can be a formidable challenge
            to work through inadequacies and insecurities

Weaknesses are indiscriminate
Is there a better time to be alive besides
confronting fears?

                I will always remember how you made me feel
                        I have not felt that way since
                  I don't know, if I'll ever feel that way again

I pray for extended seasons of peace
I dread those long moments of terror

         Tears fall, blood is spilled
           lies defile beautiful lips
    smoking guns spend indiscriminate rounds

How could it end so horribly wrong?
By appearance, it all began so wonderfully right

              I am searching for a hill to die on
     I will not be, a coward slain straddling the fence

If it all made sense, it would be too easy
if I were complete, there would be no need to overcome,
there would be no reason to grow or advance

          Sometimes I feel like I'm circling the same route
                              in the middle of nowhere
               miles away from, I wish you were here

Audition

I stand ten toes down
chest out, chin up

I'm not ashamed to say that I am blessed
no, not to be confused with luck

Animus is promoted
between men and women
condemnation overshadows love

Blood boils in my veins
many beatings have made me tough

Be encouraged if you're struggling
don't you quit – keep trying

Social media has filters
to make us comfortable with lying

I abhor all these agendas
and seeing so many babies dying

We need straight answers from those elected
and less deflecting, word salad, and denying

I laugh in the face of terror
while on the inside, I'm crying

Family over everything
too much time was lost

It was expensive when vows were broken
the children struggled to pay the cost

The moon and stars light my path
I can see well in the dark

If you aspire to wear a crown
be prepared to bear a cross

Temptation stays close
She's ready whenever she calls

Every day sees new victims
I ask you,
Is there not a cause?

Broken crutch

My body craves rest on this silent night
the stars and crescent moon, shine behind thick clouds
my many thoughts flow at a rapid pace

        Here, I lay another long night alone
        the only time I ever felt at home
        was in the soft place deep inside of you

                The only time I ever felt safe
                was while being held by you
        calmed and reassured by your sweet caress

Your fingertips would glide
all around my shoulders to the nape of my neck
and end up buried deep in my hair

Sometimes, boundaries are crossed
and needed bridges are torched
and sometimes there's just no going back

And we relive precious memories
filled with pleasures of good times
pleasant days and remarkable nights

To balance all the foul reminisces
distasteful experiences, unfair realities
and vain imaginations

Vivid, insane, and or graphic
as they may or may not be

Seconds left

Back in the day
you and I would often promise forever

Unfortunately, forever was a beautiful lie

Some bonds grow super deep,
defying logic and odds

Some bonds, through pressure
and circumstance become undone

There are also bonds that get shattered
and in its aftermath, bitterness scars
tainting good sentiment

Was it an obsession, a deep connection
or do I still love you?

It is an awful shame
that we haven't corresponded in years

But life is life
and our brief space in time ended long ago

Besides the meteorologist's prediction,
I don't know much about tomorrow

All the magic in the world
can't bring me back to yesterday

This very moment,
you dance in my thoughts

I smile as I enjoy the last seconds of a song
that we used to be so fond of

And I am perfectly fine
with being a part of a beautiful lie

Sequel

I was naive to consider a few as friends
not knowing secretly, they considered me a threat

                    I tried creating beautiful memories,
                    the end result, was years of regret

It is a waste of time
to dwell on what I lack,
I am grateful for all that I have

                    Working against an invisible clock
                I encourage myself to complete this task

Tough losses are crucial
for they humble and properly put in place,
a balanced ego fosters a healthy esteem

                The sun rises on the dawn of better days,
              I reap well in this season of positive returns
              I won't undermine it through lust or greed

Sometimes, I am discouraged
Sometimes, I vibrate high
Sometimes, in dreams I experience a different life

I hate when the pulpit is used to line pockets
supporting fake prophets, teaching false doctrines with
lies

Suffer not the innocent
Angels protect the weak from falling prey
to cunning seductions of predatory deceit

Love is power, hate contaminates,
what's visible on the surface
often contrasts with what lies beneath

I see the world for what it is
I catch myself day-dreaming of how it could be
I won't pretend, it's someplace it's not

Death is undefeated,
collecting souls without prejudice
regardless of how powerful they were,
or how hard they fought

Oh, Hell No!

For just a moment,
right before I felt the dagger
cut deep into my fifth rib
and rip through my sternum

    I was lacking as we snuggled, basking in calmness,
        it was blissful, all cuddled up with you

                I was actually content,
    while your full lips made gentle circles on my chest

But, after I kissed your forehead
and to my surprise, your cold, open eyes
locked with mine

I knew it was all a lie
I knew I was in grave danger,
disgusted by the realization that I played myself

      Choking on my own blood
      I hate myself for giving heed to my heart
      and throwing logic to the wind

            The very same logic that I ignored
            in the ruse of accepting you,
            for exactly what I knew you were all along

I struggle to think of a worse death
while taking my last breath,
than to die as a capable fool…

Prayer

Heavenly Father,
I thank you for blessing me
to live to see another day

I thank you,
for your covering and protection
that got me through yesterday

And I ask,
for your covering and protection
to get me through the rest of this day

God,
I give you praise,
all glory and honor

In your matchless
and Most High name I pray
Amen

Tactics

Mass dysfunction is profitable
                trillions are made off of war

The exchange for me donating to a grifters cash app
                is being taken for a fool once more

I don't fear dying
    I fear dying from self contempt, for not fulfilling my dream

I would choose to evade laughing hyenas,
    than to be a chipmunk in an open field, beneath a red-tails screech

Deescalating a situation is underrated
               that ability may save your life

However, once a situation escalates
    it would behoove to be well prepared, to kill, outrun, or fight

Thirteen to one

I am a part of the thirteen percent
I'm aware of the thirteenth amendment
I danced with the devil on Friday the thirteenth

I often think of death
maybe then I'll fly
when all I see is white
I simply close my eyes

Many lost their lives being brave
many gave up their freedom
for choosing violence to address disrespect

If there is a hell
I reckon most of us will probably burn

And if there is heaven,
Whom among us is righteous enough to enter?

Systematic this or cancel that
I feel like…
on second thought, never mind

I concede; the floor is yours
What would you like to talk about?

Well, if you insist,
What's good, everybody?
Everyone calls me Nate

I am a part of the thirteen percent
I'm aware of the thirteenth amendment
to my detriment, I danced with the devil on Friday the thirteenth

Wait What?

I am sure that I will finish this marathon
simultaneously, I struggle with doubt

So I run on like a sentence,
respect boundaries or get run over

I can not run forever
Eventually, I will run out

Out of strength
out of time
out of touch

As years swiftly pass
I will have come and gone like the wind

I work hard at a dead-end job
but this dead-end job pays

I couldn't be happier that I left
she loathes me because I did not stay

Love will
Love is
Love won't

I gave my word
I know I could
wait, no I don't

The one thing we all have in common
is, someday we all die

Once I learned how you could betray me
I didn't feel the need to know why

Diary

Quiet as I keep it and as talented as I am,
from time to time my intrusive thoughts interrogate
and sometimes in those moments, I question my worth

Personal accountability is one of the motivating factors
that assist me to grind so hard

Talent is only as good as talent can produce
consistency, a strong worth ethic, and timing
change the game

I am forever chasing "you"
I have no desire to be the best
I want the respect of the "best"

I feel like I'm running out of time
and as badly as I want to help the world,
right now, it's imperative that I help myself

It's a damn shame
that whenever she wears that blue dress,
I just can't help myself at all

My guilty pleasure is my attraction to darkness
but I love God and always will
so, I have no infatuation or fright of any fiend

It was a fun three years
but I lost my sense of direction
three years is a long time to be distracted

Fight or flight could get me killed
especially if I don't have the sense
to be scared enough to run

Rest in peace Jay, part of me feels
like I owe it to you to achieve greatness
before it is my turn, to crossover to the other side

Cancerous culture

To me, cancel culture is a cancer culture

        Many churches care less about God
         reverence is held for traditions and culture

If the vulture's trap is exposed
and I decide to enter the trap and get caught,
Is that on me? Or does the blame fall on the vulture?

        I'm staring down forty-six
        no explanations, no excuses, no fear

Season after season, I got caught in a cycle
but I decided nope, not this year

        I don't wear a mask, so I can't let you get close
        A haters foul energy is quite contagious

If I have to sell my soul for you to know who I am
I'll stay irrelevant and never be famous

I study to be quiet
through consequence, I grew slow to anger
I'd rather lead with love than rule with wrath

        As long as I stay in the presence of God
        I am safe from Satan's grasp

I tell stories, lyrics create anthems,
I share poems, I write songs

        I pray for a virtuous woman with a loving heart
        feminine, friendly, and fit

God, you gave me the words;
use me as a conduit to help someone through this gift

Slow Burn

Through the infinite span of eternity
do you ever wonder,
what will be remembered of you?

If spirits are recycled
and change wars with what remains,
I believe creators inspire future creators
to create something new

I've tolerated more than I should have
I seek forgiveness for more than I deserve
through cause and effect, I've garnered justifiable disdain

Feelings grew deep
the fallout was devastating
all the time wasted cannot be regained

Storytellers paint realistic portraits with words
oftentimes the story is dark

    If one can build up strength to swim with orcas
    they will be capable of hunting sharks

        Expression, change, purpose, and pain
            gave me reasons to sing

            I can't fathom the infinite span of eternity
            After my demise,
                what will be remembered of me?

Spirit of expectation

God, if you control the winds in my life
I will give you worship

Not once did you promise it would be easy
your promise was it would be worth it

Holding on to this, I live in expectation
and labor, preparing for an "and suddenly"

I am being molded by the potter
I am being tested and tried; God has his hands on me

Thank you for never failing to carry me through
You are worthy of all praise

At times, I forgot my calling
and abandoned my journey
but I never forgot how to pray

Pain is temporary, trouble don't last always
some seasons of suffering
seem like they will not end

Some battles aren't worth fighting
I laid my burdens at the altar
and that's when my healing began

I am not perfect
I've been made whole
I am not ashamed of the gospel of Jesus Christ

Thank you for all the prayers
I appreciate the love
ya'll don't know how that saved my life

Learned a few lessons that humbled me
now I know, when to let a few things be

God, grant me endurance
when life trials are overwhelming,
remind me to keep my focus on thee

God, if you control the winds in my life
I will give you worship

Not once did you promise
it would be easy
your promise was it would be worth it

Open door

I lost another friend
no tears left to cry

You will be missed
we shared some really good times

Made sure I was up early
by the time I was ready
it was too late

Can't afford time off
don't have time to spare
My family's future is at stake

Yeah, I still think about her
we lost touch years ago

I'd prefer to apologize
than to hear, I told you so

I fear if I stop running
My beating heart might stop

You were surprised I remembered
I couldn't believe you forgot

I refuse to tarry
while the clock is running

Learning the lesson was harsh
looking back. I now find it funny

Vanity

Life has no choice
but to continue on
inevitability things change

                        No matter how much
I accomplish in this life
future generations will not know my name

Happiness has not been
a good friend to me
avoiding me, as if I were a venomous kiss

                    A great first-time usually gets chased
a heart for God compels men to repent

Discipline, consistency
and good character
maximizes abilities, talents, and gifts

                  If a counter punchers timing is off
he risks getting knocked out by a lights out hit

Power has been used for terrible evil
often abused by the insecure

                      The devil that I know is viscous
but I'd rather not meet the devil
lurking behind that locked door

In Need

I take heed to the clench in my stomach
the acceleration in my breathing
and slight tightening in my chest

An ominous energy assails my spirit
follicles rise on the back of my neck

I pray for blessings to fall from heaven
like heavy rain drops

One love conquers hate
and all this killing stops

And to have less crime scenes
and plenty more weddings

An abundance of healing of trauma
families would thrive together

Division grows deeper
God is in control,
even when trouble, is all I see

Who doesn't want followers?
viral moments create opportunities
love fights for those in need

The path narrows as I climb higher
I have sacrificed to fully enjoy what happens next

I pray I have fun
I pray I make a positive difference
with whatever time I have left

What's it worth?

What if the universe stepped in
when God took rest and decided,
  everything will now come with a price?

    And nature carried that motion
    weaving death into the cycle of life

      The more I seek
      I find, there's more that I don't know

  If I have a good day,
  unhealthy sleep cycles disrupt my night

I am addicted to this game
I may never win

    And if by some miracle I do
    that victory will undoubtedly
    come at a price

Within

Bats feed on fireflies
a copperhead devoured a rat

Two pit bulls battle, both are mauled
a squirrel is detached by a feral cat

                                          Misery solicits company
                                the truth is forced to stand alone

                                            Failure teaches how to win
                              prayer and love guide lost souls home

A storm is brewing out on the ocean
while a devastating fire makes ashes of trees

Faith over fear, facts prove feelings to be irrelevant
smiling faces are known to deceive

                              The cocoon holds a wonderful transition
                              the beautiful monarch grows in its sheath

                                  A spider's web is a strange kitchen,
                                    Who works harder, an ant or a bee?

Yokes of oppression shackle spirits
I won't let life beat me down to my knees

Hate grows as I spread love
keep me nearer my God to thee

                                      For I have hope beyond reality
                      I sprint through a gauntlet with desperate faith

                      Portals are open, discernment is valuable
                                      danger lies in wait

I am not as far as I should be
I'm a thousand miles from where I was

Life is a gift; an expiration is guaranteed
I hope this vessel is empty, when my time comes

Early Autumn

Rest in peace. Tito Jackson,
Frankie Beverly and James Earl Jones

> It was a wild weekend, for sure
> be that as it may,
> My Saints are 2-0

Two failed hit jobs?
Why are his enemies so desperate to silence his voice?
fake news makes me question – what is real?

> RFK Jr. switching sides was shocking,
> similar to when Prime Time
> signed with the Niners

Poor Tim's family don't even rock with him like that

Do you agree with major resources being allocated
to provide for non citizens in this country and abroad?

Look at all the multi-colored flags waving all over
How many of them are red, white, and blue?

> What an interesting time to be an American!
> It was a wild weekend, for sure

But the weekend is over, now I must get back to work
Rest in peace, James Earl Jones, Frankie Beverly, and Tito
Jackson!

Yeah that's right

Wise enough to peep something's amiss
Keen enough to sense
it will get much worse

Experienced enough to stay out of the way
Love you enough to leave you alone

Strong enough to give you a pass
Kind enough to offer my last

Understood awhile ago that
this is all bigger than me

Tough enough to handle the pain
Fast enough to successfully get away

Slick enough to pull it off
Nimble enough to do it one more time

Confident enough to talk my shit
with enough game to never ever
have to steal a kiss

Another day

If you'll allow me to end on a happier note

I am pleased to announce that today is Angies birthday
and someone bought in delicious cookies
from Crumbl in honor of her special day

I'd also like to add, even though I wanted to,
I did not choke the life out of a prick who shall remain
nameless
and in my mind, would have rightly deserved it

Not only that,
but this being the twelfth day of the new year marks
fourteen days sober for me

If anyone cares, I feel better physically and spiritually,
mentally, I am getting my ass whooped
but I said earlier wouldn't complain

All in all, God is great
I am grateful to testify that
I don't think about hanging myself
nearly as much as I used to

Lately,
I'm more accepting of this process to greater
and less depressed from the seasons of losses

What a blessing! I can finally look in the mirror and
not despise the gap tooth fella that faces me

I feel like life is a mixed bag
so I've learned to mix the bitter with the sweet

Anyways,
Happy birthday Angie
Wishing you many more

You know, it's kinda cool, and it has been awhile
since I ended on a happier note

She Is

Law of attraction state that opposites attract
Does synergy form
when similarities vastly outnumber differences?

Deep conversations exhume intentions,
dislikes, expectations and shared interests

In the midst of a dry season on a rough day
a sweet breath of fresh air, lit a wildfire within me

Her grand smile rivals the reflection of a sunrise
on a still quiet lake

What stands out about her besides,
great features, radiant skin, and a curvaceous frame,

Is, her high vibration energy
positively affecting anyone
in her vicinity

She executes and remains in her divine femininity
her gifted hands are nurturing
her welcoming presence shifts foul moods

When she speaks of her faith, goals
and expresses her passions,
I am tuned all the way in

Mutual respect is earned, trust gained, trust shared
and over time, we prosper on a strong foundation

So ultimately, instead of her asking, can I come over?
She'll ask, baby when will you be home?

Yes, I've fallen hard for a beautiful
black woman

And my desire is for no one else
nobody's perfect

But if there is a woman
that is created perfect for me
I have no doubt that she is!

March on

Stop looking back
Times have changed

As close as you were,
You are now strangers

Yes, unforgettable memories were made there
However, as wonderful as that place was,
It is now defunct

Perhaps better days are coming
Perhaps not,

The present will soon pass
Time is too precious to waste
I know you're hurt
March on!

A Window In Heaven

I ask myself, if a feather were to fall
from a window in heaven,
How long would it take to reach earth?

And if any of the archangels were jealous
when God made man out of dirt

I really hope it's the effects from eating junk food late,
night after night, dream after dream

At first, they were bizarre
then they kinda made sense
lately, they have been obscene

If I make it to heaven
I'll finally be made perfect
without sadness, anger, or pain

Then I'll know what it's like to behold God
I'll probably trip
the first time he calls my name

Eventually, I'd find a window,
and drop a feather
to time it's descent to earth

After that, I'll find Gabriel, Rafael, and Michael
look them in their eyes
And ask were they jealous
when God made Adam out of dirt?

Can't call it

        I mourn for what was
    I fantasize what could never be

I imagine, and in turn create
my fetish, I won't speak on

                    I don't hate you, my dear
                        we were never in love

       It's not that I'm too old to fight
    now, I have something too valuable to lose

And if I ever get caught
I'll be disappointed in myself

           Ashamed and acutely aware

That I should not have been there
in the first place

Second is runner-up to the victor
or emphasis after a point
has already been made

Maybe on my third attempt
everything will work out

I refuse to cry over time wasted
money mismanaged,
or energy not properly applied

Instead, I laugh hysterically
because I know that

There is absolutely no way
that I should be standing here in first place

Day one

I am done drinking
I will not drink
I can not drink

Whenever I drink, it's impossible to think

How I feel today
will hopefully carry over to tomorrow

Today starts my often talked about one day

With much to work on
I train through practicing my gifts
I train my body when I work out

I am not obtuse to the fact
that I have a catalog of issues to work through

Which makes me wanna drink
It's a good thing I quit drinking

Yes, I quit drinking
Because, I shouldn't drink
I said I was done drinking

I can not drink
I will not drink
I will not

I need help,
No I don't
I really need a drink

The thing is this

Revenge is always personal
the violator shapes how cruel the intent

I run like hell, but I cannot escape
I am grateful for the friends I have in low places

    When it appears that my demons have gone awol
    they arise again, again war resumes

        When the truth cuts deep,
        deflection is much easier
        than to admit fault, or get caught in a lie

            I have a sick sense of humor
            articulate monologues elicit emotion
            I work hard to come up, all I amass
            will be left to fools after I'm gone

        Still, you only live once
        it's hard to be like Jesus
        for I am told he never sinned

These last two decades, I have lost plenty
now that I an in midlife
nothing or no one can convince me that I will not win

Eclipse

What is one night through the eyes of eternity?

I seek refuge from this mad world's absurdity

Creativity lives in open fields,
clear skylines and winding streams

Stories are formed through
laughter, tears, and silent screams

If I were to dwell in zero gravity
I would have no apprehensions of falling down

Whenever I am in Tink's presence
serenity hovers heavy all around

I am so sorry, I failed you
I wanted to do right, I really tried

I do not fear crossing into the unknown
I choose to believe
freedom will accompany my demise

No such thing

Decades later,
I can relate to, when Marvin Gaye told Tom Joyner
love is misery, and marriage is miserable

In my lifetime
I found that I am either too selfish
or have seen too much

That said,
through situations, growth and understanding
I am open to fully engage

If I ever find something pure,
uncomplicated and real

Marriage, however,
is still a hard no for me

The only exception would be is
if I were lucky enough to be loved
by a woman just like you!

Yes, Beautiful, let us take a shot
Nice,
Oh, you want another?

Fine, let's toast to maybe,
one day, and what if

Sweetheart, I learned the hard way,
so please don't confuse me being a realist
for me, being a pessimist or cynical

I am a storyteller
with more years behind me
than I have years ahead

And I have yet to see a fairy tale
in real life, have a happy ending

Devil may cry

When times were "good", every day was a celebration
without a care in the world, I learned nothing
I didn't respect much, let alone myself

It was all laughs, foolery
chasing women, raising hell
and getting higher than a falcon's nuts

I drank through the "hard times"
killing my body through work
attitude was horrible, and my aura was dark

After hitting rock bottom, I gained focus,
I started to seek answers to change,
suffering brought me closer to God

And that season of tests and trials
showed me everything
I needed to know about myself

Only then did I become a man,
I had to exile myself from the pack,
and from time to time that still bothers me

To become great was intentional
I had to walk alone, to first discover
and then walk in my divine purpose

Now, I know my worth
I understand being equally yoked
devotion, sacrifice, reciprocity
and so much more

And, yes, the devil still tries
And I'm sure the devil cries

Because it lost all control
Once I conquered the devil within

Finite Bliss

How long until I am forgotten?
Will hard times eventually go away?

>I keep hearing a dog bark
>Sometimes, when I'm around others, I feel strange

Playing it safe turned out to be costly
I found thrills in taking risks

>I was turned on by her touch
>I pulled away when she moved in for a kiss

Propaganda tricks the masses
Harmful rhetoric corrupts what was once pure

>The first victory felt better than I expected
>I've lost a great deal chasing more

A good man goes unappreciated
Protective boundaries can appear as cages

>Cycles produce patterns in life
>On every continent, a war rages

Lives were lost fighting for freedom
More will die before it comes

      I hope I made the most of what God gave me
        when my life's assignment is done

It feels like I've been here before
Maybe my heart and timing weren't right

         Can I handle the pressure?
     Refrain from making emotion led decisions
         it's hard to ignore signs

I am not fond of failure
But failure and rejection
Are what kept my dreams alive

      And if I am locked out of heaven
       I will gladly settle for a cabin
     surrounded by forty acres in the sky

Unanswered

The eagle soars in the daylight
the owl hunts at night

        I pray fervently for peace
        knowing eventually, I must fight

A man who gains a full understanding
sabotages happiness
a misunderstanding can cost a man his life

        Some enjoy playing with all types of guns
        others are fascinated with a variety of knives

Whatever you do,
make sure you do it well
never ever take for granted a loyal friend

        Lies get exposed, stories unfold
        what is true comes out in the end

I don't claim to have the answers
I attempt to articulate my thoughts
as they inspire the stories I tell

        My intention was to love a good woman
        and for us to flourish
        unfortunately, that did not end well

I'd rather fail trying
then, on my deathbed
wonder what if

        I watch my step, I took the long way
        keeping me clear from all the bullshit

Nightcap

We went from thick as thieves
to so distantly far away

At this point
I don't know you at all

At best, we're strangers with memories
your absence used to be a sore spot
but it is what it is, life continues on

My heart has become colder
not an ice box
but at times, ice cold

Life is a complete story of a long journey

When one chapter is complete
another unfolds

Until the final chapter we all must face

When I die, I hope that
every memory I am featured in
runs vivid

What a perfect plan that fell awry
conned by an illusion that we were solid

Tonight,
I'm sitting here tripping
while I'm sipping

Trying to rationalize how,
we went from thick as thieves
to so distantly far away

And now,
I don't know you at all

Great escape

She has caressing soft hands
I won't be crass and speak on
what she does with that mouth
when she's submissive, I take control

I held it in until she climaxed
she likes me deep when I explode

Exploring pleasure zones, such fun times
my beard was drenched from her juicy peach

She woke up ready for another round
I broke a sweat,
putting her back to sleep

Her phone kept buzzing
and so was mine

We chose to cheat
but everybody lies

We held each other in a long embrace
and then we bid goodbye

It was a great escape
from the life I hate

I am so looking forward
to our next time

One more chance

Sometimes, I feel like I need to smoke
Other times, I don't miss it all

Some days, I feel so high up
that I belong in the clouds
Other days I imagine my downfall

I entertain suicidal thoughts
More often than I would like

I forget about her while caught in a hectic day
I long for her in the still of the night

I saw change approaching through a telescope
looks like it's trapped up there with the stars

I will not dim my light
I am thankful for how I was raised
by God's grace I made it this far

Expression is therapy to me
If I am unable to create, I will go mad

I've failed so many times
But it's like I told all the women
I inevitably let down
Baby, give me just one more chance

Free game

The distraction was the prosecution of forty-seven
The failed play was to secure an election

Refusal to submit to being led or being covered
Consequently means forfeiting protection

If I am wrong, call me out
A fool despises correction

If tithes only require ten percent
Why do congregations solicit multiple collections?

If you don't sow, it's impossible to reap
Scenes of life can be hard to watch

Greatness awaits those who prepare and execute effectively
Confidence is a key factor when facing great odds

The mighty water has receded
All praise to the Most high for bringing me through

Age has robbed me of my youthful vigor
However, my senses are sharp,
my spiritual and mental remain astute

A viral moment is a powerful speck in time
But beloved, what comes next?

Many want to be feared because their hearts hold fear
I would rather share a mutual respect

Discovery

Will you stay loyal
if I happen to fall
and suddenly, everything was gone?

The ascension was quick
confidence was built slowly
the process and struggle was long

A King being feared
has to outweigh respect or love
jealousy is a deadly threat to the throne

I had to leave everything behind
to walk alone
only then did I find my happy home

I read a lot and discovered
discrepancies in much of what
I was taught, believed, and was told

Sometimes in life
compromise might require that I bend
but integrity won't allow me to fold

Community

Big cities and small towns
provinces, counties, and districts
all strive to coexist in peace

No place is perfect

Community matters,
allow me to share what community means to me

My community
is much more than a neighborhood
it's a place I'm proud to call home

Here we celebrate
many traditions, cultures, and tribes
in honor of generations past and present

And by the grace of God, generations to come

From the babies to the elders
and the busy bodies to the knuckleheads

We don't always get it right
but we always come together if things go wrong

We endure hard times,
we also enjoy happy days
witnessing seasons come and seasons change

Here, families, friends, and neighbors form a village
making it a good place to raise children

Love, faith, and understanding combats
hate intolerance and fear

We rise and fall together
tragedies only make us stronger
sure, we have our differences

But those differences help us appreciate
all that we have in common

High school football games, cookouts
graduations, holidays, festivals,
home-goings, weddings,
kids playing in the streets

We aspire to grow and get along
there are times we argue
and sometimes, we fight

But in the end, we realize it's not that deep

Yes, we face hard times,
we also enjoy happy days
witnessing seasons come and seasons change

A community where I live, work, and belong

My community is much more than a neighborhood
it's a place I'm proud to call home

Road trip

I probably should not go any further
backtracking is not appealing at all

>Right or wrong
>be it my karma or my destiny
>I chose to be here

I wonder,
will I find answers
or will I have more questions?

>Stay the course
>or change direction?

It's getting late in the day
but the sun is still up
so, for now, time is on my side

>I'm stranded
>on an island of conflicting emotions
>well, it feels more like a lonesome town

This goes so deep, like an ocean
with so much unsaid and even more unseen

>Am I chasing?
>Hell no!
>I am driven; I'm not trapped
>but I am far from free

Backlash

Your response was cold and bitter
like an arctic wind, be that as it may
I'm glad that you answered my call

If I could do it all over again
I'd correct my ways and put you first

        In retrospect, I can now see how selfish I was
        and the ways that I made bad situations worse

        Unfortunately, none of that matters now,
        nope, not one bit of it matters; what a shame

Life goes on, and so do we
to embark on separate paths
leaving what we once shared,
now, an empty void

Well, it was great to hear your voice
and to know that you're doing well
the papers are signed, and I will be fine

        I truly understand why your response
        was cold and bitter like an arctic wind
        I'm just glad that you answered my call

Old man

Very few apologies were given to me
I've apologized more than I can remember

Even if I didn't mean it,
In most of those times
I meant well and I believed
it would make things better

Honestly,
I struggled with being honest for years

I lied to those who loved me
I lied to those who hated me
I lied to those that were honest with me

And as egregious as it was
I often lied to myself

Still, I consider myself to be a decent man
every once in awhile, I have scumbag tendencies

I pray to receive all I desire
I also pray for grace from what I deserve

Villains garner either respect or fear
conversely, heroes go unappreciated,
heroes often die before their time

I fall further behind chasing righteousness
blocking out the thought, that there's a chance
I may burn in hell

Taking the risk

I can't take those that I love with me
If they don't wanna go

>Yeshua said, come walk with me on the water
>So I stepped out of the boat

I just made it through a bad storm
A bigger one will touch down soon

>Each time God walked me through the fire
>I was not consumed

Mistakes, bad choices and hard times
are opportunities to trust God to show his hand

>The road ahead tells me that I can't
>but faith assures, undoubtedly, that I can

Stories, anthems, dreams

Fear thrusts me forward
love holds me back

I am thrilled to dive feet first
into troubled waters

Every now and again
I am pleasantly surprised

The last time I was in shock
was when I found out Jay died

Cops shocked me with a taser
years before then

Now that I'm somewhat sober
it's been easier to get up

My skin has toughened
so neither the blows
nor the knockdowns hurt as much anymore

Even if I'm going the wrong way
I am going all out

I will never fail to pray
if I stay on my square
I will not fall prey

My talent will get me a seat at the table
My character will my hold my spot

All eyes are on me
I'm not nervous at all

It is a pleasure to tell stories
through poems, anthems, and songs

Patience, Devotion, Time

When our eyes lock
it feels like that moment in time stops
specific words are unspoken through long glances

Pretty brown eyes, soft chocolate skin
and a vibrant smile that causes
a realist to behave like a romantic

Great conversations soothe hope deferred
I am so grateful for undeserved second chances

Sweet embraces lead to good night kisses
eloquent words are good
but pale in comparison to consistent actions

Some things are meant to be
some situations should never have occurred
there's much in life I do not understand

I've broken many promises
I promise that I will not stay
I could never be your man

You already know

Much of society is offended by everything
and at the same time
ashamed of nothing

                        Confidently, I turn my back to you
                            it is clear that you are bluffing

I'd rather swing first and apologize,
Then get dropped
from trepidation or reluctance

                        I will refrain from calling you
                            what we both know you are
                    Respectfully, I'll address you as beloved

I have little optimism for the future
knowing full well dark days are coming

                    Leaving me a short time to pull off one last score
                                        Are you in?

The clock is running

Did not

After I turned around, the good times had come and gone
I pray that they come back around again

> I wish I told you the impact you had on my life,
> it felt way too soon to bury you, my friend

Sixteen years of commitment
sixteen years full of lessons and sowing
sixteen years of tolerating exes when it is my turn

> The joy from creative expression is too sweet,
> the frustration from rejection slices and burns

I don't trust myself
it's harder to trust a woman
because she sets traps between her thighs

> My face hurt from laughing
> so I ran deep into the woods
> it was there I started to write

Natural selection influences the wait in the middle
staying idle too long will turn you stagnant

> I'll never tell it all, but I'm happy to explain how
> I did not become wasted talent

No promises

I won't make promises
and I require none

If I don't invite you in
I can't expect you to stay

It's hard to decipher
if this situation is a distraction
or something that I should pursue

Chemistry is undeniable
but other circumstances exist
desire enables situations to occur

I can see us growing close
but I've also seen a lot
so I am cautious how I move

Not settling for less means waiting
patience leads to wanting
rushing, opens portals to sorrow

Attraction is one thing
quality conversation is another
commonalities provide a smooth flow

It caught my attention
and I am fond of
the unique way that you say my name

As this situation plays out
I will soon discover
hopefully, without difficulty

If you're a distraction, a lesson
or an opportunity that I should pursue

Anecdotally

Interestingly enough
most of my many scars are either self-inflicted
or are the result of me catching strays

By the grace of God,
every device used to
destroy me was proven inefficient

Projections, statistics, theories, and analogies
I am open to being proven wrong

But I know I'm right
so I am confident that I won't

If inside the cell is where the devil plays
I wonder if when the Undertaker climbed to the top
He took a second to pray

High as I am
and the current state of Mankind
I wanna be thrown off, too

I know it will hurt like a son of a bitch
the taste of my own blood brings a smirk to my face

I've shed more tears from laughing,
than I ever could from anger, anguish, or a broken heart

Interestingly enough
most of my beautiful scars are either self-inflicted
or are the result of me catching strays

Nonstop

Right now, I'm doing what I'm told to
I lost the luxury of doing what I wanna do

I played in the dirt
until it turned into mud
I try to wash away the filth, just like you

I thought I was clever
I tried to ignore red flags
I was self-centered and also aloof

I drove and worked drunk
I was surely unsure
but I have never been confused

The betrayal was cold
I lost a lot

Everyday it rains karma
Will it ever stop?

Controlled environments are aggravating
for a man who lacks self control

My faith is of a decent measure
I lost hope in you awhile ago

If you succumb to her spell
her demons will fight, before they let you go

I gave you fair warning
I will be the guy to remind you, you were told

I had one chance, and I took it
with bloody feet, I run

My plan is to outrun the devil
until the angel of death comes

I have plenty of time left
but not enough time to start all over again

I've learned and adjusted
from every losing season
this season the goal is, win

We will never be together
She's the only woman I'll ever miss

I keep to myself and mind my business
and the reason is…

The betrayal was cold
I lost a lot

Frustration is mounting
 karma rains nonstop?

Short term

The catalyst to many villains' origins
are brutal injustices to decent men

Having said that,
plenty of heroes and so-called good men
fail, crash out, or get caught up

Many run to religion out of desperation
The voices in my head fall silent after several stiff drinks

        I wanted to change,
        I thought I had changed
        I really tried to change

        Ain't it funny how life unfolds?

My smile serves as a mask
It brings me joy to hear my brother's good news
God gave me grace to handle pain

I wish others blessings
as I walk through hell
privy to the fact that I wasn't sent here to stay

        That's how I know pain won't last forever
            forever is a long time
            and my time is fleeting

In forty five years a lot has transpired
I fail to remember the beginning

It probably won't end well
Conversely, I question
if it truly ends at all

Fortitude

My favorite basketball player of all time is A.I.

Should I fight or embrace this infiltrating technology known as A.I.?

>Confrontations, complexities, compromise
>she seemed so cool with her lying eyes

>Can't get as high as I used to
>yet, still I rise

It's difficult to communicate effectively
while being misunderstood

Rolled and tripped, trying to escape hard times
I miss my adolescence, when times were good

>The world is changing, I am growing older
>and further out of touch

>Although she's been dead for years
>to this day, I miss her so much

Long one

I try to imagine my spirit leaving my body
after the final breath of air escapes my lungs

I am undecided if my corpse
will be displayed in an open casket
or if my ashes will be held in an urn

Death is an unavoidable part of the circle

Only God knows when my life's assignment is done
Death is scarily fascinating

The last few that I lost where close to me
their demise brought pain and surprise but no tears

That is precisely why
I don't mind failing
each new day is a chance to get right

One day, there will be an obituary for me
And I will be ushered to wherever and
whatever comes next

Hopefully by then
I will have decided

What to do with the carcass and organs
unable to enter the next dimension

If I ruled the world

I am going to conquer the world
and leave it all to you

You should know that seclusion kept me free
from the oppressive hand of tyranny

Great fear became as much a part of me
as the blood flowing through my veins
that same great fear, I eventually faced and overcame

A legion of voices produced a million opinions
a degree of sapience could not allow me to be happy

Woe to these deadly distractions
Lies hide in plain sight, at close range,
I question, what is true?

I have lost everything and survived,
if I die in the next second
my life's body of work can not be erased

All that I've done wrong
and all the wrong done to me
inspired me to find another way

I am a simple common man
giving back what I was given

I will not bow to principalities, malevolent entities
or gluttonous jackals conspiring to rule

So beloved, when the time arrives
that I conquer this world,
I will happily leave it all to you

Facing Jericho

I admit that I was knocked down
and in retrospect, I stayed down
much longer than I should have

I felt like, maybe I aimed too high
and that my abilities, work ethic
and gifts weren't enough

And maybe, it was past time for me
to wake up from this dream
that has driven me for decades

I replayed struggles over and over in my head
I thought of times when I was a different man
with a dark plan heading in the wrong direction

And right when my foot almost slipped
and I returned to a familiar road
of anger, self-hate, hopelessness
and self-destruction

I remembered whose image I was made in
how far I've come, my undying spirit within
and how I escaped all that hell behind me

Then I got up
drank a liter of water, stretched
did some calisthenics, meditated, and prayed

Later, I picked up my pen
and unleashed these words from my soul
in some form, war will always be with us

When I'm going through hard times
I try and remember the good times
life gets tricky, some days bring bitterness
other days can be amazingly sweet

I wrote this for you; to encourage you
and I pray hard that you never give up
love is love; God help me to help others
Thank you for reminding me to encourage myself

Poker face

Some you win
and on the same coin
some you lose

Karma pays with interest
to those cheating to get ahead
so it's best to pay your dues

If you plan to change the game
you must fully comprehend all the rules

Calamities either cause you to run away
or bring out the warrior in you

The gauntlet awaits
and lays straight ahead

What am I to do?

Through time and hard work
I have prepared to win

Time and experience have also proven
that I could very well lose

Dead line

I've been up
And I've been broke

I was the man
I've been a joke

I laugh hard
No, I won't sulk

I've promised I would
And then I don't

Sometimes, I'm clutch
Sometimes, I choke

I road shotgun
I steered the boat?

The path grew dark
So I move slow

An eerie figure
Reveals a narrow road

I thought I was close
Now, I know

I had some fun
I enjoyed this show

Let me hit this bump
And then I'll go

On My Way

Confronted with hard choices
in the midst of trying times
and under pressure to make the right decisions

I rely on wit, courage
and knowledge passed down from my elders

I've never seen a man speak to a mountain and it move
although my faith is strong,
I have common sense

With defeat and disappointment behind me
my quest has brought me to my greatest challenge
I am hungry, tired, and afraid – yet I am also certain

Certain that on the other side of this mountain
is the source of all I've ever needed

Life has prepared me for this daunting task
I've come too far, just to come this far

My faith is not strong enough
to tell this mountain to move

I am hungry, tired, and afraid
but with everything that I am made of
I climb, and I climb, and I climb

Open mic

The blend is sweet music to my ears
the keyboard rivals the unrest in my soul

The saxophone screams higher and louder
the trumpet loses all control

                    The bass provide deep tones and bounce
                    the drums are a heartbeat, keeping time

                            Lyrics hit my head
                      like taking a massive bump
              relevant, aging well like a fine wine

Influenced by the greats
that came before me,
motivated by what's to come

I wanted to be successful
I felt I needed to be heard
right now, I am having fun

                  A long day led to an interesting night
                            the crowd is diverse
                      it's dark in here, but the stage is lit

                          I absorb the atmosphere
                          rhymes form in my soul
              through this open mic, I found bliss

Jaded

Maybe the reason that no one is coming to save us
is that too few are worthy of being saved

I am desensitized to the carnage around me
I smoke a dutch, unbothered and unfazed

All our heroes are dead or compromised
it will take a supervillain to ensure justice is done

It may not end well,
hell hounds have picked up my trail
rifle loaded, I am too tired to run

I don't fear baptism by fire
we are all liars
God claimed everything he made was good

I will no longer allow my feelings to get the best of me
I hate myself for omitting to do the things that I should

I kept licking and kissing even after she climaxed
hours later, my beard was filled with her scent

Days later, I broke her heart
cursing all those who come after me
to suffer from my memory's lingering stench

Strategy

Not every slight warrants an address
there are times, shut lips attain peace

Bodies of work take a lifetime,
God bless the souls
of all the lives that were cut short

Today is a decent day,
tomorrow is not promised
I often struggle to understand why I am still here

I work hard to get better,
setbacks pushed me forward
I adapted to a different way to fight

I met my soulmate during midlife
and we shared several beautiful moments in time

But those moments never grew past moments
because timing and circumstance were not right

Written word, spoken word, invisible boundaries
I let go, and once I did, creativity found me

Society has gone soft
and is ill-prepared to deal with bullies
bullies only understand violence and force

Selective outrage is a virus; procrastination aborts opportunity,
variety adds flavor to the world

It's not about what I believe
it's about what I can prove

Which makes for an interesting conversation
when faith speaks for much of what little I know

Interlude of the sad man

With so many variants created to distract or infect
I take shots while I avoid getting shot

I palm light the size of a candle
in a valley that's pitch black dark

I find it interesting that when I encourage others
the message I'm given often applies to myself

This path I travel is meant solely for me
I can't walk with anyone else

In the last decade, I've come a mighty long way
sometimes it's hard to see the light

Will my soul enter purgatory,
Heaven, or will it go nowhere at all
if I should die tonight?

Wisdom came from observation and mistakes
my endurance has been proven
and so has my heart

The saddest thing that I relive
is being a major factor
in my family being torn apart

I am in heavy competition
with the man in the mirror
only through death will this rivalry cease

I would rather
be in stable situation, than fall in love
if I were starving, I would kill to eat

Idols are constructed
to be worshiped by men
scavengers devour the carcasses of fallen beasts

It is written in scripture
It is not good for man to be alone
but sometimes, being alone
is the only way to maintain peace

Alluring situation

At this point, I choose to remain silent
if I were to state how I really felt
by saying anything more,

>It would, without doubt
>make this situation worse

>>I like the way you flick your hair back
>>and the gleam that brightens your eyes
>>whenever your attention is occupied

The way your face parts and reforms
when you display that smile,
is a wonder to behold

>This current season requires
>separation, discipline, a sober mind, and consistency
>and this season has not been easy

>>I miss those sweet things
>>that only the presence and essence
>>of a woman can provide

I have no qualms whatsoever,
regarding this temporary loss of focus

>In order to achieve my goals
>and ascend to levels I've yet to reach

>>It means the process will require much
>>from and of me

So, if you happen to catch me in a gaze
and my facial expression may appear eager
like I have something important to convey

>Please, take no offense when I turn and walk away
>I have learned the hard way at a heavy price

>>That some things are better left unsaid
>>and some situations – no matter how alluring
>>are better off left alone

Respectfully

It would be quite a stretch if I were to say
I wish I could take it all back

        I will say things would be much different
                Had I not said anything at all

The process has taken longer than I anticipated
And a greater challenge than I expected

No excuses!
No complaining!
No whining!

                I did not notice a glass ceiling
          Just clouds, the sun, stars, and moon

Love me or leave me
And if you decide to leave
Feel free to resent me too

            It's cool if you won't stand with me,
          Understand, I will treat you as a threat
        If you choose to loiter and lurk behind me

If you decide to stand in my way,
Bro, step aside or get stepped over

Happy as hell

I find it intriguing how best friends can become bitter enemies
I think it's beautiful when strangers become family
It's sad when the elders are disrespected and pushed aside

      Is there ever a good time to deliver terrible news?

Would you want to know when the last time would be
that you were to lay eyes on the one
that made you feel a way no one else could?

      Would you rather die years before your time,
         full of joy and complete, but broke as hell?

Or, outlive everyone you know
and be wealthy and also cursed
with a permanent emptiness within?

      Friendly eye contact can reach a
      dark soul
         a look of disdain can break a spirit

Hate defiles the human heart
and is a great nemesis to progress

      Every day a dream is shattered
      and some poor bastard harshly finds out
         that they aren't good enough

Life ain't fair
Damn, this world is cold

Stay

It is impossible to recall
how many times I was ready to give up
I do know that every time that feeling came
somehow, some way, I chose not to give in

I used to consider
adversity, opposition, and boundaries
as obstructions, obstacles, and problematic

But I realize now that
they are more akin to great rivals
for they are motivating factors,
forcing me to adapt, making me better

Contrary to microwave, right now culture,
good success takes great effort, failure, and time

So before you quit and walk away
from a gift that you've put so much into,

Dig your heels in deep and keep grinding
during these hard times

And perhaps we will sit next to each other
at the table when we finally make it
to share our testimonies
on how we were ready to give up

But we didn't give in
and we saw our breakthrough
as we overcame, after committing to one last try

Whiplash

I walk amongst shadows of what is to come
I drink the early morning dew
of inspiration that will eventually exhaust
hours after the sun light erases the fog

I don't fear death's angel
Nor do I fear the fallen architect

I looked them both in their eyes
one was disappointed
the other, shocked

It's only a matter of time before I utterly destroy
everything and anyone around me

No,
I will try my hardest to do right

Maybe I can convince you
that I am not a madman
and we can lie to ourselves and each other

With delusional hope
that I won't be a great disappointment
to all that love me

When I get caught up, yet again…

World wide

Peace Beloved,

Words can heal, words can also kill
guard what enters your mind, and what comes out of your mouth

I pray and work for healing, love, and prosperity to rise, multiply
and permeate all over, connecting east, west, north, and south

Freedom is an undying commitment, empathy is an ally
to change, every leader needs a cause

In spite of all the negativity we hear, feel and see
It is important that you understand
that there is a meaningful purpose to your existence.

Division is the adversary to unity; we can not stand or grow divided,
a lack of understanding has no regard for compassion

Fearful rhetoric and dangerous agendas keep us separated

Ignorance is the bloodline to hatred and hatred, of self or others will imprison us in a dark state that I abhor.

Circumstances and experiences shape one's attitude but belief in one's self defines aptitude

Through all the pain, frustration, vexation, disappointment, prayers, and hopes for a better tomorrow

Accept that feelings change; keep moving, elevating, and producing
beyond whatever adversity and or opposition you encounter

Stay positive! Be safe! Do well!
One Love

Lessons and Blessings

The path to greatness can be described as many things
easy, will never fit that description

        Finally doing the right thing when times have changed
                          is a hard lesson to learn

Even when I thought I might die from pain
the good Lord was still blessing

                          I will never be perfect,
               I have no ambition to attempt to get close

Good and evil can be argued from perspectives
I'd rather fight to be righteous, being made in the image of God

> I ain't taking shit from anybody
> I won't take what a man worked hard for

Predators devour without a conscience
My people need help
so I refuse to take advantage

> And if in the event that my tomorrow does not come
> I prayed for this message to find you

Make no excuses; understand life is not only seasonal
but sometimes cyclical

> Greatness is much more than what you accomplish
> It's also defined by how you inspire. uplift and put on
> without benefit or incentive

Conditioned

Fundamentals are vastly underrated
being fundamentally sound can dictate
an outcome of a fight

Scriptures caution us to work while the sun shines
However,
I am behind, so I must also labor at night

I have appreciation
for wisdom gained through participation
great wisdom is priceless when freely given

I want to be loved fiercely
without restraints, ulterior motives, or conditions

The tables are turning
situations are working out
I am healed where I once was broken

My spirit is free
my body is in shape, and my mind is open

Unfaced fear can drive a man to do many things
unbridled anger can cause him to ruin his life

Years of disrespect will make
even the kindest hearts explode
anxiety makes days dark with sunlight

I am thankful for all the wisdom I've gained
I appreciate the wisdom received, while freely given

I hope to one day be loved fiercely
by the woman that I love

without restraints, ulterior motives, or conditions

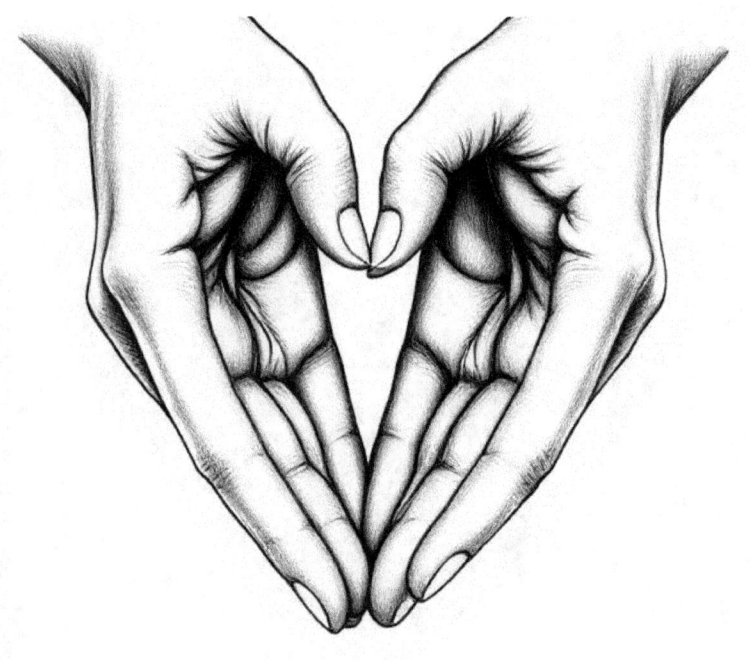

Eulogy

I have always thought that
memorial services and funerals serve the living
I'm at peace to be remembered
however, I am remembered

Be that good, extreme, and or foul

I would hope that my ashes aren't kept or spread
instead, throw the whole urn
into a blazing bonfire

If I am not meant to have the fortune
to enter eternal paradise
Or, if mercy would see fit
that I am not included to burn forever

It would be fair if,
my soul were to never take rest,
but fed, by the unseen consequences of all I did wrong

Eternally bound to the aftermaths of everything
I was too much of a coward to get right

If my spirit is allowed to live on,
let it be an avenger

Benevolent to the pure in heart
and malevolent to those
that truly deserve it

Or, maybe it would be better to have my entire existence
carved in granite between 1979 and whatever year
I am released from this physical form

Born Again

Sometimes when life is unfair, it's difficult to recognize
that somebody has it worse

    We like to operate in our gifts
    but find it hard to admit if we incur a curse

I don't mind being a team player
but I work best alone

    All I want is a Nissan Titan, a double-wide
    and if I'm blessed, a slim, thick wife
    to help make it a happy home

I am not asking
I am not going back
If I stop we won't eat

So long for now, I have much work to do
    I'll see you again when it's time to feast

And if I am cast into the lake of fire
I hope God tells me
I'm sorry, son, I know how hard you tried

Growing up I heard the devil being blamed for everything
      yet, it is man who steals, kills, and lies

I'm not obligated to explain what I believe
I just know what I know

      My heart is numb, my intentions are pure
      and I've let some dead things go

Introverts can possess extrovert tendencies
Adapt, evolve, or perish in these last and evil days

      It doesn't matter how I feel
      What matters is that I stand as a man
      And face whatever life sends my way

Clarity cuts

To think clearly, I had to cut some things out
to find peace, I had to cut some people off
after I got sober, I stopped cutting up

I am closer to the age of sixty than I am to twenty

Now that I'm finally on the right path
I'd be lying if I said I didn't worry
if time has passed me by

Everyday, I move forward
and with each attempt
I get better

I have no time to celebrate
any measures of success
or to appreciate how far I've come

Although with diligence, I stick to the plan
progressing through the process,

I cannot deny or overlook
the fact that I am closer to sixty
then I am to twenty

Samantha's smile

Some days are good
Some days are hard to tell

Beloved nothing is promised
I hope you're happy and doing well

Enjoy your journey
Fly high enough to kiss the stars

Always keep your head up
Especially when times are hard

Walk in your purpose
I pray you see your power
there's a process to greatness

Keep grinding, growing, and shining
Smile, Samantha, you gon make it!

The Grave Equator

Feelings arise and pass
similar to steam released
from a hot spring

Feelings can not always be trusted
for the simple fact that feelings change

I've never cared more
than I care right now

I've been close many times before
each devastating loss
was not easy to overcome

Somehow, by the grace of God
and sheer determination
I continue on, over and over again

Retain, comprehend, and application
three of the many keys
that are imperative in my life

Life is full of
milestones and tipping points
often times, critical mass proceeds mass destruction

I wonder if the grave is an equator
between Heaven and Hell?

I can say with conviction
that I have never cared more
than I care right now

Maybe I am misguided
maybe I'm fighting a battle I shall not win
Maybe I am wrong

In remembrance of

I drink Tequila whenever I remember
Jack Daniel's when I try to forget

Celebrate memories of good times past
I pass out on nights that I lament

If I didn't earn it, what did I gain?
Most things that are given, can easily be taken back

A good personality, a solid work ethic, and consistency
can make up for attributes one lacks

How is it possible to be an aggressor
and a victim at the same time?

Karma's contingency plan for those who escape it
is reserved for descendants through bloodlines

The only reason that I loved you so hard
was because I hated myself

From time to time
I relive the worst pain
I have ever felt

God hated Esau; God also forgives
diabolical dominion will not be redeemed

He kept starting fights
but we all knew he was drunk
He might still be alive, if we didn't make him leave

Tequila, whenever I remember
Jack Daniels, when I try to forget

Celebrate memories of good times past
I pass out the nights that I lament

Pretty eyes

She offered a view, into her soul
as I gazed deep into her pretty eyes

                        She said she was being honest with me
                        but I already knew that she kept secrets
                                       and told many lies

Tests, trials, opposition, and seductions
have made me strong, perceptive, and wise

                                    I empathize with losers,
                              I have sympathy for almost
                      but quitters and complainers I despise

Sentiments and desires pass
like the going out
and coming in of a tide

  Somethings will never change
  we experienced ecstasy under a full moon
  And again right before sun rise

  When she said, I love you,
    I laughed to myself
    while looking deep into her pretty eyes

Get Ready

If I were to be granted a rather
I would rather not be here

And if hell meant
I could laugh no more forever

It makes sense that in heaven
there would be no tears

Since I must endure hard times
I pray my good seasons go by slow

The way the earth is spinning
I will not cease praying in the days to come

Good and evil can be indoctrinated from a perspective
then again, good and evil can be absolute

No, is a complete sentence
being told no can be used as motivation
to blaze trails and knock down doors

I hope you fulfill your potential
I hope you make a significant difference
I hope you choose, you!

Reasons

If I cut you out of my life
please know that I did everything within in my power
to keep you in, including hurting myself

I turned my back and detached
from all emotion and affection, for my own safety,
peace and overall well-being

If I ever let you go
that decision was for your benefit
the truth is, you dodged a bullet

Now,
if I ever did you dirty

Well, one of two realities apply to that unpleasantness

On one hand, I'm sorry, you didn't deserve it
I was a selfish, degenerate
inconsiderate, reckless idiot

But trust that karma has dealt with me accordingly
and has painfully paid or currently paying me back in full

Now, on the other hand,
You and I both know you deservedly had it coming

And in that case
if I could do it all over again
I would change nothing
I would change nothing at all

Summer

Whenever I ask,
How do you want it?

Your answer is always,
"More than less"

Some days are good
some days are worse than others
Today is already a test

I prayed, did a few sets,
then enjoyed a cup of coffee
smoked a blunt and got my mind right

Even with the lights off
a glow illuminates the walls
compliments from the early sunrise

I am locked in
with a solid plan in motion
everything will work out soon

I walk down the hall,
bedroom door is wide open
my eyes are happy to fall on you

Wrapped in a towel, no cosmetics
skin glistening, hair wet

Rubbing lotion on your legs…
a wonderful memory,
that ultimately leads to regret

I stood there numb from shock
as I watched her casket
be lowered into the ground

She tried to love me
I failed trying to love her back
Real talk,
the way we ended was foul

Our first time was such a sweet time
but 99 in the summertime
without a doubt, was the best of times

We were inseparable that incredible summer
we had so much fun, but sometimes
 I'd rather not remember

We broke up on Friday the thirteenth
she was murdered three days later
just before Fall, on that bloody September

Sometimes the memories cause grief
at least those moments were exciting, full of laughter,
and often affectionate, loving, and tender

I wish I would have apologized,
she didn't get a chance to look back,
I will never forget that beautiful Summer
And now, I am so cold
every day feels like winter

Anti

I would prefer to be chosen by God
than to ever be summoned

To escape hell, I had to fight like a demon
once I realized no angels were coming

Save you or save me?
Even Jesus can't save us all

We waste our free will on what feels good
feeding our flesh when our starving spirit calls

I ain't a preacher, I am a follower of Christ
I'm not completely sure what being Christian means

It ain't about race it's about class
the only color that matters is green

Blood is shed for diamonds, lies coverup
bloody hands rob and kill for gold

It's easy to cause chaos; it's easy to destroy
it's damn near impossible for us to stay on code

I have a big imagination
I often ponder, "What if?"
I am too old to pretend

Each year that passes by
more morals are shed
the scariest monsters are men

Paradox

It's difficult to acknowledge
the times I got it right

                                        While being haunted
                                by all that I have done wrong

I find encouragement
and also rebuke
when I analyze the book of proverbs

                                    I find common ground
                                      with pain and praise,
                            when I study the book of psalms

Remaining silent through exhaustion
while feeling beat down
unfairly paints me as morose

                                                However,
                                    The more I endure
                the closer I get to what God has in store for me

As my eyesight diminishes
I know that if I go blind,
the vision will continue to be seen

Never

If I ignore my conscious in the moment,
my misdeeds may be uncovered years later
karma's voice of retribution too loud to ignore

Why does it disturb me
after I hurt those who conspired to hurt me?

Why does my faith and trust remain in God,
when aligning with Satan is heavily lauded?

Instead of comparing
Why not prepare?

Why beg for attention,
when you create a space?

Where do I find the strength to keep fighting
when over the past two decades
I have fell-short over and over again?

What has already been done
plays a strong hand in how I go forward

If God is omnipresent, all knowing, and omnipotent
Why would he be offended by my many questions?

I am pained by the memories
of those that did not make it

The spot that I hold was not offered
so I had to take it

When the good old days arrive
I hope I am in a position to enjoy them,
I pray to God that they last

Old dog barking

It benefits me nothing to tear my brother down
it benefits the collective when we find common ground

If the authoritative power becomes oppressive, we must resist
to revive productivity after a decline, spark a catalyst

Offering new perspective to a period in time, situation, or point of view

Bad seasons won't negate the better days to come
I enjoy where I'm going but can't forget where I came from

We entered a "golden era" with a house divided
the fight is fixed and the deck is stacked

I agree to disagree and even if we never agree
I can debate opposing points of views,
without hurling insults and verbal attacks

When God says, nah, not yet
that is the time to do what is needed to better ourselves

Some days, I want to life to return to how it used to be
some weeks, I don't wanna be around anyone else

Always read body language,
connect three sides to find the truth
listen to understand, know when to respond

Tribalism officers a safe place
everybody needs a space where they belong

Love note

To the beautiful woman that I cherish,
If our love is to be tested and tried
through seasons of hard times,

    Know, all that I feel for and about you will not falter
    I am blessed to live
    this incredible life with you

        Not long after entering your life,
        It was clear, that you were the woman
        that Almighty God made for me

    It has been quite a journey thus far
    we've experienced good, bad
    and a whole lot in between

        Yet here we stand, face to face
        eyes locked under God, seeking him
        in whatever comes next

Baby, I appreciate you
You are the love of my life
Oh, just so you know

    Soon as I get home,
    you gon get it
    And I can't wait!

Against the flow

I chose hope
and now grow effectively

Forced to create boundaries
society crumbles collectively

Faith keeps me grounded
I am comfortable
marching against the flow

It's true that nothing lasts forever
Absence seeks residence in my soul

I won't allow bad elements around me
to infect the joyous harmony within

I climbed up out of a downward spiral
so cycles of elevation could begin

Even the foulest of men can do good things
good men aren't immune
to committing evil deeds

Predators know how to read a room
attention feeds low esteem

Both Liberals and Conservatives can be off putting,
rhetoric from both sides flood streams and feeds

I enjoy hiking trails in the woods
I miss being in the sanctuary to witness
melodies fall from heaven as the choir sings

Becoming

Every day I work to be a better man
I am no longer the man that I once was

I have not yet fully become
The man that I will be

At first it was fun,
after awhile it was unfulfilling

Day drinking led to nightcaps
years go by too fast to be wasted
changing direction was the only logical course

later, I acquired an appreciation for routine and silence,

I have entered the proving grounds
I am ready
This time, I will overcome

God forgive me for my sins
Cover me, guide me and keep me
Lord, have mercy on us all

I could be wrong

I'm not sure if I know what I'm looking for

I am too old to be seeking validation.
Aren't I?

Why is it that every time
I decide I am done drinking, out of nowhere
I am struck with incredible thirst?

Why do I exude confidence when I have nothing?
How is it that I keep creating in the face of rejection?

There's a difference between being lonely and being alone
things got better, right after they couldn't get any worse

I often feel like I'm wasting time
    I work too hard to be remembered as wasted talent

    What is kept locked up, will eventually try to escape
    I broke the spell – if you weren't there, I will never tell

    In the past greed and a closed mind
    kept me off-center,
    it is a blessing that instability is no longer a problem

    If happiness starts within,
    maybe I am better off seeking peace

    I'm not sure what the hell I'm looking for
    I just pray to God that I find whatever it is
    before time passes me by

Past time

Fatigued and close to drowning in my own thoughts,
daylight threw me a life raft

Then as quickly as a blink of an eye
I became numb
to feel nothing at all

Three days passed
before I accepted the stark reality

That I might not
feel anything again

To this day, I question
if that was when the mind trap was dismantled
or inspiration was sprung

Peace

Greetings Beloved,

I am grateful to be alive and in tune to create.

It was fun putting this volume together. I was blessed with a variety of interactions and experiences to help shape this book. The themes, issues, and ideas written throughout this manuscript covered a broad range, including faith, doubt, poor choices, consequences, regret, hope, hypocrisy, and flaws in human nature. Healthy spiritual and mental balances inspired a full spectrum of thoughts, imagination, and emotions, which were a pleasure to express and share.

I am honored that you chose to walk on this journey with me. I hope you enjoyed the trip and that something in this book spoke to you. I appreciate your support! There's more to come!

God Bless You
One love!

Nathaniel Terrell

Publications

Broken crutch
    First published in *The Blunt Space Incorporated*

Timeline
    First published in *Men's Today Magazine*

Open Mic
    First published in *Jerry Jazz Musician*

Seconds left
    First published in *Kaytell Ink*

She Is
    First published in Kaytell Ink

Another day
    First published in *Friday Night Library Magazine*

Worldwide
    First published in *Waxing Phoenix Gallery*

Free game
    First published in *Poetry Catalog*

From the diary of wasted talent
    First published in *Pen to Print Publishing*

Within
    First published in *Oddball Magazine*

On my way
    First published in *Manic World Magazine*

Clarity cuts
    First published in *Pockets Literary Journal*

Love note
    First published in *Voice & Virtue Literary Journal*

Acknowledgments

All praise and honor to God for blessing me with this talent, determination, and resilience to create. Without God, I am nothing.

Thank you to my wonderful parents, **Trellis** and **Saundra Jones**, for your unconditional love and for raising me right. I love you both more than I can express. I am forever grateful for your support and patience(even after I lost my way). I appreciate all you've done for me and my siblings and the many sacrifices you both have made. Much of who and what I am is because of your prayers, good upbringing, and the Christ-like example you've embodied to this day! I hope I made you proud.

David Burton – The Last Podcast

David Burton is a devoted child of God, a passionate writer, and a transformational coach dedicated to helping others unlock their fullest potential.

    http://thelastpodcast.info/
    http://www.youtube.com/@TheLastPodcast-cs5jx

Robyn

Waxing Phoenix Gallery is a platform for multiple genres & multiple skill levels. WPG is dedicated to the support & growth of all artists.

    https://www.waxingphoenixgallery.com/
    https://www.instagram.com/waxingphoenixgallery/

Kayla Tellington – Kaytell Ink Publishing

KayTell Ink Publishing is a small but undeniably growing literary magazine with a primary focus on showcasing new voices and providing a bridge into the publishing world.

https://www.instagram.com/kaytellpublishing/

https://www.instagram.com/kaytellpublishing/

KAYTELL INK
PUBLISHING

Amy Stein – R.E.F. Rochester Education Foundation

Their mission is to collaborate with educators, businesses, and the community to form and maintain partnerships to fill resource gaps and programs to provide meaningful experiences and improve learning and success for all Rochester city students.

Rochestereducation.org

info@rochestereducation.org

Mikael Carlson – Warrington Publishing

Working with you was a great experience. I appreciate your effort and, taking the time to break down facets of the publishing process that I was not privy to. And also explaining while showing what it takes to make this book a success. Thank you! I look forward to the next project. Salute.

Samantha Scantlebury(I am proud of you! Keep growing and shining!)
Author, Editor, Owner
SYS- Survive Your Struggle Clothing
https://sysclothinglondon.com/

Chris Jones
The Life Writing Podcast on Youtube.
Lifewriting.com   website
Chris "CJ" Jones, A.K.A. Mr. Life Writing, is the Founder, Managing Member, and Chief Editor of LifeWriting.com. Its mission is to produce mediums that inform and inspire people to write the lives they desire. The mediums are captured via The Life Writing Blog and The Life Writing Podcast. Follow him across social media @MrLifeWriting.

About the Author

Nathaniel Terrell is a poet, storyteller, author, and artist. In 2021, Atmosphere Press published a collection of his poems, titled, *Is there not a cause?*

He also creates spoken word videos and inspirational shorts for his YouTube channel, Instagram, and X pages.

More of Nathaniel's work has been published in Maudlin House, Retrograde Review, Lifewriting.com, Christian Creative Magazine, Mas Magazine, Nine Cloud Journal, ChristArt, and more.

Feel free to follow, connect or subscribe to his website, pages and channels:

Youtube	@natejstory4994
X	@NateJstory
Instagram	@natej.story
Linkedin	www.linkedin.com/in/natejstory
Email	wastedtalent79@yahoo.com
Website	www.natejstory.com

www.ingramcontent.com/pod-product-compliance
Lightning Source LLC
Chambersburg PA
CBHW070104080526
44586CB00013B/1176